A HISTORY
of
COLERAIN TOWNSHIP

From
Frontier Wilderness
to
Suburban Sprawl

Joe Flickinger

HERITAGE BOOKS
2018

HERITAGE BOOKS
AN IMPRINT OF HERITAGE BOOKS, INC.

Books, CDs, and more—Worldwide

For our listing of thousands of titles see our website
at
www.HeritageBooks.com

Published 2018 by
HERITAGE BOOKS, INC.
Publishing Division
5810 Ruatan Street
Berwyn Heights, Md. 20740

Copyright © 2018 Joe Flickinger

Heritage Books by the author:

*A Bicentennial History of Green Township:
Uncovering a Jewel in the Crown of the Queen City, 1809–2009*

A History of Colerain Township: From Frontier Wilderness to Suburban Sprawl

Cover Photo: Colerain Township Memorial Plaza
Photo courtesy of Mary Burdett

All rights reserved. No part of this book may be reproduced or transmitted in any form or by any means, electronic or mechanical, including photocopying, recording or by any information storage and retrieval system without written permission from the author, except for the inclusion of brief quotations in a review.

International Standard Book Number
Paperbound: 978-0-7884-5804-0

Dedication

This book is dedicated to my wife Kathleen and our children, Erin, Ryan, and Kelsey.

Table of Contents

List of Illustrations...vii-viii

Foreword...ix

Acknowledgements...xi

Introduction ...xiii-xiv

CHAPTER 1: Shawnee Hunting Ground to Colerain Township...1

CHAPTER 2: Early Life...19

CHAPTER 3: The Birth of Township Communities...31

CHAPTER 4: The Twentieth Century Brings Changes...47

CHAPTER 5: Post-War Growth: Farms to Subdivisions...65

CHAPTER 6: Looking Ahead to the Future...95

Appendix...107-110

Bibliography...113-116

Index...119-120

List of Illustrations

1. Ft. Dunlap
2. 1856 Map
3. 1869 Map
4. Hardin House
5. West Home
6. Colerain Population
7. Giles Richardson Trough
8. Water Trough Inscription
9. William Maner on Farm
10. Colerain Ave. Looking North
11. Morgan Heritage Trail Sign
12. Intersection of Colerain Ave and Struble
13. Colerain and Galbraith 1910
14. Groesbeck Hotel
15. Colerain and Galbraith 1906
16. Hotel Keller
17. Creedville Toll House
18. Dunlap Cemetery Stone
19. Memorial Service Brochure
20. 1990's Dunlap Ceremony
21. Bevis Cedar Grove Vault
22. 1856 Railroad Map
23. Mt. Healthy Airport
24. Lakewood Airport
25. St Bernard Church
26. Constable John Willsey
27. Anti-Thieving Badge
28. Colerain-Springfield Anti-Thieving Badge
29. Groesbeck Fire Badge
30. Groesbeck Fire Department
31. Dunlap Fire Department
32. Cornerstone Flyer Colerain Schools
33. Colerain Consolidated School
34. One-Two School House Districts
35. Pleasant Run School
36. Blue Rock School
37. Colerain Bus
38. 1st Graduation Program

39. Colerain HS Photo
40. Northwest HS Photo
41. Northwest District Population
42. New Pleasant Elem.
43. Rumpke Truck
44. Neidhard-Minges Funeral Home
45. Donauschwaben Hall & Clubhouse
46. Farbach-Werner Park
47. John Stehlin and Truck
48. Fort Dunlap Marker

Foreword

Welcome to Colerain Township!

History is only as important as it is available. This book, *A History of Colerain Township: From Frontier Wilderness to Suburban Sprawl*, makes the history of our township available to ALL of us. The book shares the beginning of area settlement: Dunlap's Station and the Village of Coleraine, to all of the communities and areas that make Colerain Township special in many ways today. The growth of Colerain Township demonstrates the life and times of the 18th, 19th, 20th, and the 21st century. Celebrating 200 years is a milestone... continuing to move forward for Colerain Township citizens is...Making History!

Reading this book will provide you with an understanding of how the township came to be, developed as it has and encourage YOU to become involved in making the history of our next 200 years. (And don't forget about that disappearing "e"!) Thank you to Joe Flickinger for the hard work he put towards writing this book. It was a pleasure to see the book develop, contribute to it, and now celebrate its completion.

With appreciation from all of us at the Coleraine Historical Society,

Mary Burdett
President,
The Coleraine Historical Society

Acknowledgements

I would like to thank the Coleraine Historical Society and especially its president, Mary Burdett, for her help and support in this endeavor. Her knowledge and the seemingly unending archives at their museum helped me tremendously in completing this book. Thank you to everyone who submitted pictures and anecdotes. My former students, who took my Local History elective, encouraged me to write a book on local history. Without your support and encouragement, I would never have tried to write, much less consider researching a topic as big as this book. To my parents, William and Nancy Flickinger, who passed their love of books, and writing on to me, I hope this book continues to make you very proud. I would also like to thank Mike Owens, Bob Decher, Dennis Haskamp, Paul Ruffing, Julie Carpenter, Patrick Olvey, and John Stehlin, for their help and assistance with writing this book. Finally, to the people of Colerain Township; may this book pique your interest in your local history; it is a wide and varied history and worthy of continued study.

Introduction

    Colerain Township has always held fond memories for me as a young boy. My mother took us to Northgate Mall to find any number of items we couldn't find in neighboring Green Township. I marveled at the number of stores that seemed to have everything! I remember sitting in heavy traffic as we exited the highway. During peak times, my mom drove what she called "the back roads" to avoid the traffic. I was struck by the rural nature of the area. Driving along Springdale Road, I saw cows, horses, and seemingly innumerable productive farm fields. These rural scenes are still visible in the township today.
    As suburban sprawl creeps further into the township, the rural character is slowly disappearing. Sleepy villages and hamlets have become bustling and thriving communities to support township residents. Colerain Township was established in 1794 and its establishment pre-dates Ohio becoming a state in 1803. What would John Dunlap, who helped survey the area, think of the township now? Would he think that his dreams of establishing a thriving community were realized? What would Jesse Bevis think of the busy community today compared to the rural village where he lived? How about the schoolmasters of the one and two room schools? Public education has evolved to serve a student population of over 9,000 students. Teachers are using technology to give "virtual reality" field trips for students to experience walking around famous sites throughout the world. What would they think of the changes since the days of only learning the basics of reading and math? While the obvious answer is amazement and maybe even disbelief, I think they would be proud of the Colerain Township of today. Residents live in a vibrant growing community, boasting it has one of the largest populations in the state of Ohio.

This book is more than a look back at the history of an area. Colerain Township is one of many suburban areas that boomed with development after WWII. The rapid growth, aided by housing developments, affordable cars, and good schools, has helped the township to continue to grow and reinvent itself for the changing times. This book celebrates where the area was, and allows the reader to keep in context the past while informing the future. It is my hope that you can sit with relatives, children, grandchildren, or neighbors and reminisce about the places of the past, while looking forward to the future. Perhaps you can tell them about the area before developers built "the mall", or what it was like watching small bi-planes take off from the Mt. Healthy Airport. I hope you enjoy this look back into the history of Colerain Township and that it sparks an interest in local history. Colerain Township is very lucky to have an active historical society that operates a museum and is active in historic preservation. Consider attending one of their meetings. Join and volunteer. The preservation of history would not be possible without the efforts of the countless volunteers in this organization.

Join me as we take a trip back in time to a Colerain Township covered in forests with lush vegetation and trickling streams, to a modern suburban community with all the amenities of a large city. I hope you enjoy the book.

Chapter One:
Shawnee Hunting Ground to Colerain Township

Colerain Township and its encompassing communities are well known to their inhabitants, but not as well known to many native Cincinnatians unfamiliar with the western side of Cincinnati. Colerain, as native Cincinnatians know it, can be a puzzle to many "outsiders" because of its unique closeness and its small town feel within ten miles of a major Midwestern city. Many outsiders venture into Colerain to visit friends and relatives, or attend community events, and emerge surprised and befuddled by the unique names of streets, neighborhoods, and community institutions. The Colerain Township of today bears little resemblance to the Colerain Township of pioneer days when Native Americans considered this area their "sacred hunting ground". The Colerain Township of pioneer days was a frontier land, far removed from the small settlement known to many as Losantiville (Cincinnati today); Colerain Township was dotted with beautiful trickling streams abundant with many types of fish and lands filled with other wildlife such as deer, rabbits, and the occasional bear or two. The Colerain Township of the late 1700's also had lush, thick forests, making travel through the area by wagon almost impossible unless old Native American trails were followed.   Travel on foot or horseback was an absolute necessity, as many of these old trails were less than five feet wide, making settlement in the area very, very slow.

To understand the slow settlement of Colerain Township, one must understand many of the obstacles in the way of the early settlers of the area. The Native Americans in the area, the Shawnee, were very hostile towards a white settlement in the land north of the Ohio as they considered the Ohio Country as their "sacred hunting ground." At first, many white hunters and trappers navigated their way through the area and made positive contact with the Shawnee and other tribes living in the Ohio Country.

These hunters and trappers hunted for a few months, bartered and traded with the local tribes, and moved on in short order. This contact occurred until the end of the American Revolution when the Proclamation of 1763 was repealed, the settlement opened to just about anyone who wished to move to the newly opened "wild west." The Proclamation of 1763 forbade any further settlement into the Ohio territory by British subjects, but this did not stop some of the travelers. Many individuals were lured to this new "wild west" by the idea of making a fresh start, a new beginning where they could make a substantial change in their life. Despite the Proclamation of 1763, settlement increased, with many individuals choosing the Ohio Valley as an excellent place to start over. Many of these settlers were native Virginians, choosing to stay Virginians by settling in the Ohio Valley. Virginia claimed a large chunk of the Ohio Territory. Many of the Virginians who moved here believed that the British Royal agents who oversaw Virginia were not going to pay attention to the movement. This inattention was in large part due to the large distance between the main urban areas of eastern Virginia and the Ohio territory.

During the American Revolution, the Ohio Territory became an area of contention for both colonists and Native Americans. Some settlers saw the region as a bastion of opportunity that was theirs for the taking. Native Americans became disenfranchised by the breaking of the Proclamation of 1763 by the American colonists. Soon the Native Americans became very sympathetic towards the British cause. Many Native Americans saw the vast, lush wilderness that they considered their sacred hunting ground being destroyed by the methods used by the new eastern transplants to establish their homes. Colonists stripped the land, with little to no regard for the environment around them. Trees that were hundreds of years old quickly disappeared and were replaced by open fields. By the end of the American Revolution, Colerain Township was still an untamed wilderness, but things were about to change. While the founding fathers were meeting back east to create a new American Government, a few pioneers were making their way to the Ohio Territory by way of the Cumberland Gap and the newly organized territory of Kentucky. Word began to trickle back east about the beauty and abundance of the Ohio Country. One of these individuals who heard of the potential for growth and profit was a man named Benjamin Stites. Stites made several trips into the area, and decided to enlist the help of others in his quest to settle and profit from this "wild west."

An important individual to the history of Colerain Township, who was also synonymous with the settlement of Cincinnati was John Cleves Symmes. Symmes was a delegate to the Continental Congress and judge from New Jersey in 1788 when he acquired over 311,000 acres from Congress.[1] In November of that year, Stites and a small group of settlers made their way down the Ohio River on flatboats and settled in what is today the eastern suburb of Cincinnati named Columbia-Tusculum. Stites and his settlers named their settlement Columbia. In December of that year, Robert Patterson and Mathias Denman led a second group of settlers down the Ohio River and landed at what is now the Public Landing area of the riverfront of Cincinnati. They named their tiny settlement Losantiville. In 1789, Symmes himself made his way down the river with a third group of settlers and landed west of the Losantiville site, and Symmes named his settlement North Bend, for the steep northern bend the river takes on its way west to the Mississippi River.[2]

Settlement was slow in the territory known as the Northwest Territory, due in part to the hostile actions taken by the native tribes in the area. In 1790, due to increasing fears of the Shawnee tribes, the United States Army was directed by President George Washington to erect a fort for the protection of US citizens settling the

---

[1] Silberstein, Iola, *Cincinnati, Then and Now*, Cincinnati, League of Women Voters, 1982 10.
[2] Silberstein, 9-10

area. Fort Washington was built to hold over 200 troops and serve as a warning to all native tribes considering attacks. Due to the presence of the fort, settlement remained along the riverfront. Settlement would remain there after a pioneer outpost called Fort Dunlap (in what would later be named Colerain Township) was attacked near the Great Miami River in January 1791. Shawnee forces led by Simon Girty, and reportedly Blue Jacket, numbering over 300 surrounded and laid siege to the fort which was manned by federal regulars and an officer from Ft. Washington.[3]

An attack on the new settlement

John Dunlap figured believed he had a promising financial payoff coming. He was convinced that the land he had plotted out was going to provide a huge financial reward for the money he had paid to his now former employer, John Cleves Symmes. He didn't realize, or maybe it didn't matter to him, that the Native Americans in the area had other ideas. This was their land, and nobody had a right to take it. When John Dunlap laid out the village he named Coleraine after his hometown in his native Ireland, he had dreams of helping to establish a very large, robust settlement. The land seemed good enough. It was located in what was then a flat area close to a large bend in the Great Miami River. It was 15 miles upstream from the Ohio River. It also was roughly 15 miles from the nearest military outpost, Fort Washington, located in what is now today downtown Cincinnati.[4] Jacob Kingsbury, a Lieutenant assigned to Fort Washington under the command of General Harmar, was sent to the small fort in early January of 1791. He had 18 Federal Regular Troops under his command. Word had been sent to Fort Washington that two settlers near Fort Dunlap had been taken prisoner by a small

---

[3] Kramb, Edwin A. *Buckeye battlefields*. Springboro, OH: Valhalla Press, 2006.
[4] Kramb, 106

Indian war party earlier in December 1790.[5] Lt. Kingsbury was sent to help protect the Americans living in this wilderness where a real perceived danger was lurking for these pioneers. Early in January 1791 the troops arrived to set up their quarters and began the task of setting up a real military outpost, which the soldiers called Dunlap's Station. What the troops didn't know was that the situation was going to heat up rather quickly in the chilly early January air.

On January 8th, 1791, a survey party of four settlers ventured to the other side of the Great Miami River and was attacked by a Native American war party. One American was killed in the attack, one was captured, and the other two were able to escape to Fort Dunlap. When Lt. Kingsbury was told of the situation, he led a small party across the river to find the dead man and bury him. They also surveyed the area and when they did not find any other signs of the Native American war party, decided it was a random encounter, and they should not be worried.[6] At half-past seven on the morning of January 10th, the Native American war party of between 200-400 warriors surrounded the fort. They made their presence known by presenting their captured American, Abner Hunt, and making him plead to the inhabitants of the fort for them to surrender.[7] When Lt. Kingsbury informed the natives that the fort had no intention of surrendering and that they had plenty of food and supplies to last for days, the fighting began. The Native Americans led a half-hearted assault but were beaten back by the troops and inhabitants of the fort. It was at this point the Native Americans began torturing their prisoner in full view of the settlers. The Native Americans led more half-hearted assaults with the hopes

---

[5] Wells, Ruth, *Colerain Township Revisited, 1794-1994*. Cincinnati Ohio, Colerain Township Historical Society, 1994, 8
[6] Kramb, 107
[7] *Cincinnati: An Urban Sourcebook Volume 2*. Cincinnati Ohio, Cincinnati Historical Society, 1988, 7

that the settlers would surrender under the pressure attacks from the warriors, and the screams of their fellow settler. The troops and settlers led a very successful defense of the fort throughout the day and into the night. Abner Hunt ceased screaming sometime after midnight.[8] Earlier in the evening, the Native American warriors tried burning the fort by using flaming arrows.[9] On January 11th, the Native American forces tried one more assault, and after being beaten back by Lt. Kingsbury and his troops, retreated into the forest.[10] Later that day, a detachment of 38 Federal Troops arrived at the fort after being alerted by a fort inhabitant, John Wallace, and a soldier, William Wiseman, who escaped in the middle of the night down the Great Miami River by canoe to Fort Washington in Losantiville.[11] The relief troops were led by Captain Alexander Truman and were accompanied by volunteer troops from both Columbia and Losantiville.[12] They found the soldiers and settlers safe and secure. Only one person was wounded in the fighting, and not very seriously injured as they were still able to assist in the fighting.

    Despite the arrival of reinforcements from Fort Washington to help secure the area, settlement almost stopped in what would later become neighboring communities such as Green Township or Delhi Township. Many of the inhabitants of Fort Dunlap moved to nearby North Bend or Losantiville, and soon and soon they disbanded the military garrison and the troops went back to Losantiville and Fort Washington. The settlers lost around 75 head of cattle, and 1,500 bushels of corn because of the attack on the fort. Militia and regular army had been sent to try to fortify the "station" as it had

---

[8] Kramb, 107
[9] Urban Sourcebook, 7
[10] Kramb, 108
[11] Cone, Stephen Decater, "Indian Attack on Fort Dunlap." *Ohio History*. Ohio Historical Society. 1887, 69
[12] Wells, 8

been referred to besides a fort, but quickly returned to Losantiville after finding the settlement of Coleraine all but abandoned.[13]

Colerain Township would be a hunter's paradise today if left untouched by the eventual development throughout the years. But once the Indians were banished from Ohio with the signing of the Treaty of Greenville in 1795, the hunters, trappers, and Native Americans knew Colerain Township would change forever. The establishment of roads would completely change the area. One of the largest and still well traveled routes today is Colerain Pike, which became known as one of the most well-macadamized roads in the rural areas of the county.[14] Many other routes, settlements, and farms were established after the creation of the State of Ohio in 1803.

John Dunlap was mentioned previously in the Siege of Fort Dunlap. He was considered to be one the most trusted surveyors for John Cleves Symmes. He was also regarded as one of the first settlers to venture into the land. He was Irish and named the area after his home area in Ireland. He arrived in 1790 and helped clear a site along the banks of the Great Miami River, which he hoped to lay out like his hometown in Ireland. He was quickly joined by a few settlers, who helped him build a small cluster of cabins closely situated behind what was considered an eight-foot tall stockade made of small timber or logs split and thrust into the ground. They built small blockhouses at the corners of the square

---

[13] Scamyhorn, Richard, and John Steinle. Stockades in the Wilderness: The Frontier Defenses & Settlements of Southwestern Ohio, 1788-1795. Dayton, Ohio: Landfall Press, 1986, 71

[14] Ford, Henry and Kate, *History of Hamilton County Ohio with Illustrations and Biographical Sketches*, Cleveland Ohio, L.A. Williams Publishers, 1881, 255

that was formed by the stockade.[15] John Dunlap later moved to Illinois and thrived in surveying.

Colerain Township Established

Before Colerain Township was able to support permanent settlers, the Congress of the United States set up rules for governing and dividing what people called the public domain. The Land Ordinance of 1785 created the guidelines for the shape and character of what would be called Colerain Township. According to the Land Ordinance, the land was to be divided into six-mile, square townships created by lines running north and south and intersecting at right angles with east/west lines. Townships were to be arranged in north/south rows called ranges. Most townships were to be subdivided into 36 one mile square sections. Each range, township and section were to be numbered in a regular, consistent sequence. [16] Unlike most of Ohio, the Symmes Purchase was a big mixture of townships divided in different directions. Some are laid out in east to west fashion. These are called fractional ranges.

As the Symmes purchase was first settled in 1788, the area was split into three distinct towns: Columbia, Losantiville, and Miami. These townships were three huge areas encompassing almost all of what is now modern Hamilton County. These three areas were formed from the three original settlements of the Symmes Purchase. These three areas were: Columbia, settled by Benjamin Stites in November 1788;, Losantiville, settled in late December 1788, and North Bend, established by John Cleves Symmes in 1789. The Colerain Township we know of today had its roots in portions of the original Miami and Losantiville townships. Losantiville became known as Cincinnati Township after the Governor of the

---

[15] Ford, 256
[16] Knepper, Dr. George, *The Official Ohio Lands Book*, Columbus Ohio, Auditor of the State of Ohio Publication, 2002, 13-16

Northwest Territory, Arthur St. Claire, visited Losantiville and renamed it Cincinnati. Another reason for St. Claire's visit was the establishment of a county, which they named Hamilton, in honor of the current Treasury Secretary and Revolutionary War hero, Alexander Hamilton. In 1795, South Bend Township was established to accommodate the brand new settlement close to what is now Anderson Ferry, by Timothy Symmes, who was the only full brother of John Cleves Symmes. North Bend was touted by John Cleves Symmes as the future home of the metropolis of the purchase area, because of its central location. This idea was supported by a detachment of 21 Federal Troops stationed there for a short time before the establishment of Fort Washington. Unfortunately, the area grew undesirable when flood waters forced the abandonment of the settlement to higher ground until the waters subsided. Much of the Symmes Purchase area remained loosely organized, remaining huge townships, while most of the attention for settlement was given to Cincinnati after the establishment of Ft. Washington. South Bend Township included all of Delhi Township and most of Green Township.

Small sections of today's northern Green Township were claimed by Colerain Township, which was formed in 1794 by the Court of General Quarter Sessions of Peace. These civic divisions changed in 1803 when Ohio was admitted to the United States as the 17th State. This is when sources indicate that Hamilton County began to shrink, as many newer counties were formed from Hamilton County. These newer counties included Butler and Warren counties to the north, and Clermont County to the east. Hamilton County, came very close to the shape it is today. From this point, surveyors began carving up Hamilton County into the various different townships as outlined in the Land Ordinance of 1785. Colerain Township's borders are somewhat different today from the early 1800's. An example of the differences in borders is the loss of sections of the township to Green and Springfield townships, while other portions left the township to form Mt. Healthy.

While no known account exists of the first trustees or their meetings, a modern source indicates a possible clue to the beginning of the townships of modern Hamilton County. The state law stipulated that once a suitable amount of men wanted to establish a government, the County Constable must call a meeting and he helped choose a chairman of the meeting. He was given orders to arrest anyone who disturbed the meeting. Fifteen male taxpayers had to be present, and they in turn elected officials by secret ballot. These officials consisted of three or more trustees, two overseers of the poor, three fence viewers, two appraisers of houses, one lister of property and a number of supervisors of land. In those days, holding office was not considered an honor. After being elected to office, anyone refusing was fined $5. By 1831 it was reduced to a fine of $2. After 1850, the offices paid too much to be refused.[17]

Today, the Colerain Township slate of elected officials consists of three township trustees and a fiscal officer. They all run for office using modern political campaigns, and are voted on by all township residents who are at least 18 years old and registered to vote. Any other positions within township administration are voted upon by the trustees, and many of the jobs, including the police and fire departments, use modern civil service examinations to produce the best and brightest candidates for possible approval by the township trustees.[18]

So what happened to the "e" at the end of Colerain?

A spelling of Colerain Township in the early 1800's included an "e" at the end of the name. This puzzles

---

[17] Scully, Henry, ed, *Remember When...Monfort Heights*, Cincinnati Ohio, Monfort Heights Civic Association, 1977, 19
[18] Colerain Township Webpage, (accessed 3/26/2014) http://www.colerain.org

many visitors and lifelong residents. Many believe it to be a misspelling when they encounter it. Some speculate about the mysterious "e" and its meaning. However, this mystery is easily solved. The surveyor of the area, John Dunlap was a native of the town of Coleraine Ireland. It is located in the Modern British territory named Northern Ireland, around 55 miles northwest of the City of Belfast in County Londonderry. Coleraine is taken from the Irish Cu'il Rathain, which means "nook of the ferns." [19] John Dunlap felt strongly about his native land, so strongly that he named his new settlement after his beloved Ireland. It is not known when or why the "e" was dropped from the name, other than it was an "Americanization" of the Irish Coleraine. The small fort which was attacked by Native Americans along the Great Miami River is sometimes labeled as Ft. Dunlap "at Colerain". The small village in the north of the township also shared the name Colerain, as does the major road through the township. Coleraine Historical Society still uses the "e" in their title, and is one of the few modern examples of the old spelling in use today.

---

[19] Flanaghan, Deirdre & Laurence; *Irish Place Names*. Gill & Macmillan, 2002, 194

This photo shows how Ft. Dunlap may have looked along the banks of the Great Miami River. Coleraine Historical Society member Robert Muehlenhard built the model from information based on written descriptions and old sketches of Fort Dunlap. The model in the photo is on permanent display at the Coleraine Historical Society Museum located on Springdale Rd. (Photo courtesy Coleraine Historical Society)

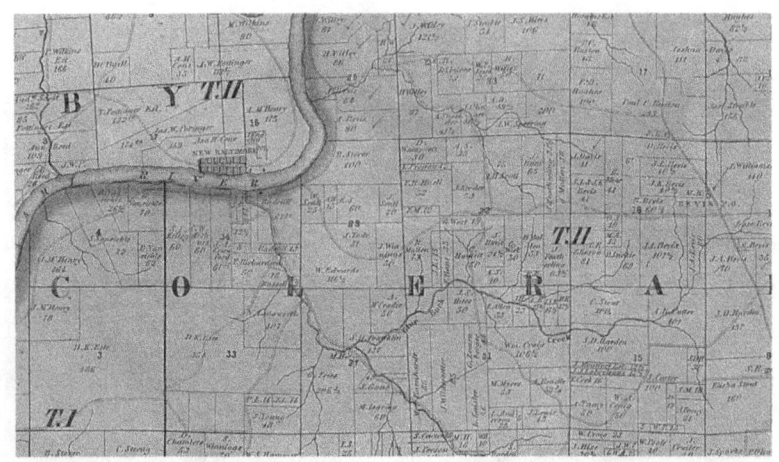

This map from 1856 shows the township divided up into square "sections", from which land was further surveyed and sold. Much of the township in this map is farms or undeveloped countryside. (Map courtesy Coleraine Historical Society)

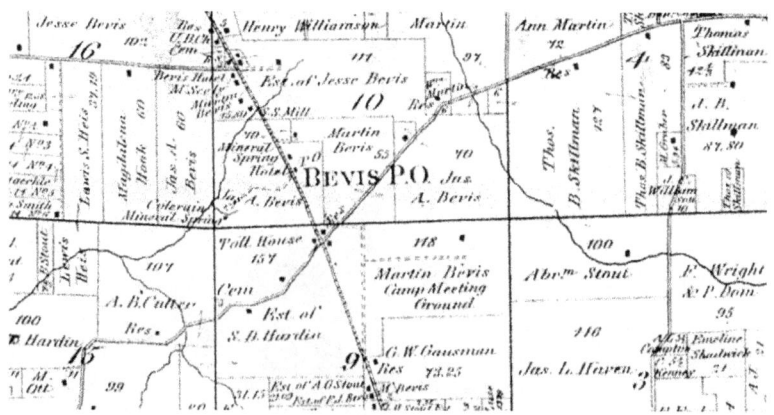

This 1869 map shows Bevis as a small collection of homes and farms along Colerain Pike. Today, the area is a heavily built up suburb with homes, condos, and businesses. (Map courtesy Coleraine Historical Society)

This photo shows the Hardin house on Springdale Road across from Northgate Mall. Built by Samuel Hardin around 1841, this home was later used for local businesses. In 2016 the building was demolished for further development along Springdale Road. (Photo courtesy Coleraine Historical Society)

This photo shows another home from early Colerain History. This is the Charles and Rebecca West home on Colerain Ave, built in the 1820's. Groesbeck was originally named West Union after the West family. After it was determinedby the post office there was another West Union Ohio, the community changed its name to Groesbeck. This site has been developed into a shopping center which includes Walmart. (Photo courtesy Coleraine Historical Society)

**Chapter Two:
Early Life**

As mentioned before, the Colerain Township of today is very different from the Colerain Township of yesterday. In today's world of cell phones, computers, and HDTV, the average 21st-century individual would find the frontier life of Fort Dunlap very hard indeed. Most would say it is very quiet, and in the case of Colerain Township, very lonely. Most of the settlers had to begin fresh wherever they went. They would have to clear the land and at the same time finish a permanent dwelling as quickly as possible. Without a permanent dwelling, life in Colerain Township was next to impossible.

When settlers arrived, the first task was the establishment of shelter. Since most of the individuals who made their way to Colerain Township first were the men, a quick lean-to was the cheap and speedy solution to the shelter issue. Families would later join the men after a more permanent shelter was underway or finished. Many of these first cabins were neither fancy nor comfortable. Scores of the early settlers found the fear of Indian attack to be a frightening idea and sought comfort in numbers. Fort Dunlap served this purpose well in the initial days of the township, especially before the defeat of Native Americans further north near Detroit and Toledo, which helped usher in the Treaty of Greenville in 1795. These pioneer cabins near the fort were not very big. Many families lived, slept, and ate in the same room. Children ran around all day never putting on a pair of shoes in the spring, summer, and fall. Farmers spent a majority of their first year clearing the land for use as fields to grow their crops. Next was the establishment of a reliable water supply. Countless township creeks and streams provided the water necessary to grow the crops as well as quench the thirst of the growing population. An early example is the establishment of Fort Dunlap near the Great Miami River- not only did it provide adequate water for the settlers, but a reliable way to transport goods down river to the Ohio River. Often the seasons dictated what was grown. Throughout the growing season fruits such as cherries, peaches, apples, and melons were grown and farmers either sold immediately at one of the many markets in Cincinnati, were consumed by the family, or made into preserves. Vegetables such as cabbage, onions, tomatoes and various varieties of corn were grown and farmers either used the food on the farm or sold the crops at the market. In the early days, farmers organized one trip per week to Cincinnati, due to the distance and roads into the city. Sometimes, the overabundance of certain crops would lead to their disposal in the city waterways on their way home. Phillip Steinman III recounted in his book "Beechwood Flats" about often having to dump excess crops such as tomatoes into the Mill Creek because everyone had bought their fill. According to Steinman, even the ketchup factories would not take the tomatoes, and since they had more than their fair share back on the farm, they would just dump them in the water![20]

Rural Living takes shape

In the early times, news was spread by communications between the neighbors. Without the aid of cell phones or computers, much of the "instant messaging" between friends was accomplished by a fast ride by horseback from neighbor to neighbor. Consequently, much of the news was old news by the time it reached the farmers of Colerain Township. The only events that were spread quickly were deaths or births. Often a member of large families would hop on the swiftest horse to inform the neighbors and friends of the big event. Many of the neighbors were close by since many of the farms and homesteads were small at 40 acres or less. As a bonus, many of the people who lived nearby

---

[20] Steinman III, Phillip, *Beechwood Flats*, (New York NY, Vantage Press, 1960) 17

were not only neighbors but relatives as well. One such instance was the Bevis family, along Colerain Pike in the Colerain Township area by the same name, Bevis. Many of the houses and some of the rural character built into them are still evident in today's Colerain Township.

By the 1850 census, the United States was a burgeoning country, with the main cities such as New York, Philadelphia, Baltimore, Pittsburgh, and Cincinnati ruling the countryside they straddled. In 1848, a major revolution in an area of Europe known today as Germany sent a large influx of German settlers and refugees into the Cincinnati area.[21] From early on, the amount of farms and subsequent little villages began to multiply. Most of the small villages became names on a map from the increased population and its shift to the west. Add in the 48'ers and the subsequent German immigration, and you have a recipe for a stable almost steady flow of traffic to the outlying rural communities of Colerain Township. If one were to meet one of these individuals, one might find the individual German of Cincinnati would have fulfilled a certain stereotype set down by many native-born Americans. Many Germans were described as having heavy beards and wearing a different hat than other Americans. These immigrants were highly thought of for their competence in business affairs and frugal natures, which gained the respect of immigrants and native-born Americans all over Cincinnati.[22] Many attribute thrift and competence to the way many of the rural farmers lived. Many were not overly wealthy but were simple and thrift individuals. Once travelers made their way to the West Fork Creek at the base of what is now Colerain Ave., they did not see the sprawling neighborhoods associated with today's suburbs in Colerain Township.

---

[21] Tolzmann, Don Heinrich, *German Heritage Guide to the Greater Cincinnati Area,* Milford Ohio, Little Miami Publishing, 2003, 13

[22] Tolzmann, 14

One would see the wide-open, fresh air of country living. Life was very slow, and to some, very monotonous. However, this way of life did have some rewards. Many of these farmers made their way to Cincinnati to sell their goods in the many markets throughout the city's neighborhoods. Others loaded up their wagons and ventured into College Hill or Clifton to sell their goods. Many farmers drove their cattle, pigs, and other livestock through the muddied roads into the city for the many slaughterhouses that made up a vital piece of the Cincinnati economy in the 1800's. Even though the population was small compared to Cincinnati, Colerain Township was a very necessary cog in the industrial machine called Cincinnati. Life was slow but very rewarding indeed.

  Often, various activities broke up the monotony of the daily grind. One activity was the breaking of wild horses that had been delivered to the different farmers.[23] Another distraction occurred when the wayward traveling salesman was chased up the nearest tree by the family dog. Many families preferred Bulldogs or Newfoundland's as the family pets due to their protective nature. These traveling salesmen sold needles, thread, and other various sundry items that the farms needed but couldn't justify a day's journey into Cincinnati. The salesmen went from farm to farm selling essentials. One of the very significant facts about the nature of the families and farmers is that they would often invite the salesman to eat with them after quelling the upset guard dogs that patrolled these old farms.[24] This fact informs the 21st-century person of the goodwill and good nature of the pioneer farmers during the early days of the township. The farmers and their communities were closely knit, and the families were even closer. Even though this rural way of life may have given way to suburban developments, the close ties that people feel

---

[23] Steinman, 20
[24] Steinman, 21-22

towards Colerain Township persist, a very real connection and pride to the area that many communities of today lack.

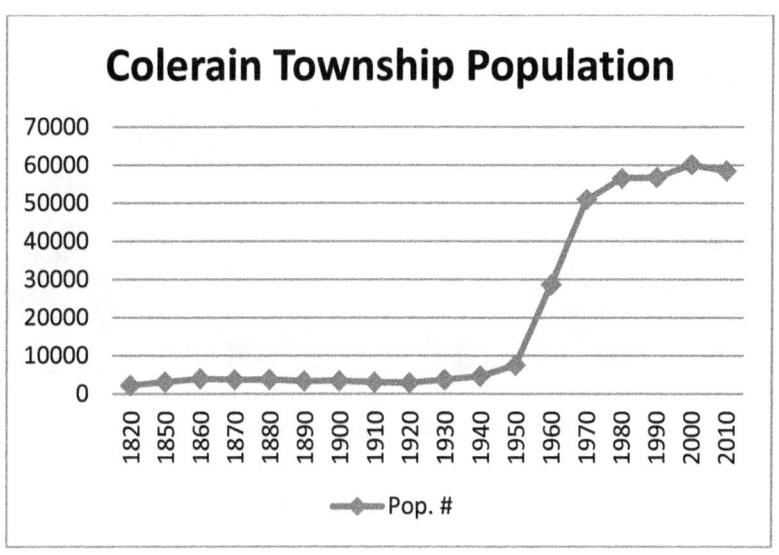

This chart shows the census data for Colerain Township beginning in 1820. Notice how the population nearly triples after 1950 when the baby boom hit the area after WWII. Farms were bought by developers to build housing for returning soldiers after WWII. Affordable automobiles provided a quick commute to work in the cities. (Data courtesy Coleraine Historical Society)

In 1867, Giles Richardson, an early township resident, installed this watering trough on old Colerain Ave. Above the spring fed water trough is a marble slab with an inscription from a John Greenleaf Whittier poem. An Ohio Historical Marker identifies the site. (Photo courtesy Coleraine Historical Society)

This marble slab located above the water trough on old Colerain Ave. contains the inscription "Stranger and traveler, Drink freely and bestow, A kindly thought on him, Who bade this fountain flow, Yet hath no other claim, Than as the minister, Of blessing in God's name, Drink in peace and go". This is from the poem "On a Fountain: For Dorothea L. Dix". The state installed a marker in 2006, calling attention to the water trough. (Photo courtesy Coleraine Historical Society)

This photo shows William C. Maner, a farmer on Blue Rock Rd. in Peach Grove, with "Coalie", the horse, mowing with a sickle bar mower. Sights like these have become fewer as the township becomes more developed. (Photo courtesy Mary Burdett)

This photo shows the intersection of Dry Ridge Road and Colerain Ave looking North in the late 1950's. Bevis-Cedar Grove Cemetery and the Old Methodist Church is in the upper left. Construction of Interstate 275 transformed this sleepy looking outpost in later decades. (Photo courtesy Coleraine Historical Society)

Chapter Three:
The Birth of Township Communities

The Colerain Township from the 1820's to the early 1920's was a growing community; however, compared to the city of Cincinnati, the growth occurred at a snail's pace. Life moved leisurely, and many of the distinct communities sprang up from the frontier as a place where the farmers could visit to get supplies from the shops and vendors who set up businesses to sell their wares in these new rural hamlets. These communities, many with no legal borders, give names to today's township areas.

Life in these regions was unhurried, and it seemed the outside world bypassed these parts of Hamilton County without a second thought. Word that William Henry Harrison from nearby North bend was elected as the ninth president and died a month after taking office was slow to reach the area. Colerain Township residents knew about the planting of crops and tending to animals; events such as the election and death of a president were worlds away.

While issues and problems began to rise and create tensions in the country over the issue of slavery, life pushed on without much thought or debate on the issue. Why should it? Slavery was never allowed in the old Northwest Territory. In 1803, Ohio was admitted to the country as a free state. The farmers and ranchers in these hamlets were hard workers who toiled on the land and reaped the benefits. As the Civil War raged on, various sons, brothers, and fathers went off to war and returned changed by the experience. They were a little more hardened, quieter and subdued than before they left. Some individuals never made it home alive; their families grieved, but life moved on; it had to, there was work to do. Colerain Township sent some of its sons and fathers to faraway places and events like the Mexican War, the Boxer Rebellion, the Spanish-American War, and World War One, the Great War. While all of these major world events were raging, life in Colerain Township stayed relatively the same. These people were tied to the land, and, as a result, toed to the seasons as well. Spring brought the tilling and planting. Summer brought the raising of the crops and the first small harvests. Fall necessitated the major harvest and preparations for winter. Winter saw life slow to a crawl. With the breaking of winter and transition into spring, the cycle started over again. In the midst of all this, each community developed a unique character all its own. While they each had different origins and beginnings, they all have one factor in common: they are all Colerain Township communities.

Dunlap

Dunlap is one of the oldest communities in Colerain Township. Originally named Georgetown and established in 1829, this community was named for the chief early settler in the township, John Dunlap.[25] It was located roughly on Colerain Pike close to Kemper and Dunlap roads. It appears the original community, Georgetown, is named after George Struble, a hotel operator and the owner of a farm close to the village. The name Dunlap originates from the original postmaster of the village, John Dunlap. He was postmaster in the old Colerain village(which had largely disappeared by the 1880's) down along the Great Miami River in an old cotton mill. When the post office moved up the hill to Georgetown, the village took on that name, Dunlap. One of the dangers of the area was fire. The Dunlap/Georgetown area experienced several instances of major fires throughout its early years. A fire caused over $5,000 of damage in an 1887 edition of the Venice Graphic.[26] Bucket Brigades were the norm for the area, and many different fires ravaged different structures throughout the community. The area did not have

---

[25] Wells, 17
[26] "A $5000 Blaze." *The Venice Graphic* (Venice Ohio), September 16, 1887.

regular fire service until the Dunlap Volunteer Fire Department was established in 1954.[27]

Groesbeck

This community of Groesbeck is located at the intersection of Galbraith and Colerain Ave in Colerain Township. A lay minister named Charles West donated some land for several churches in the area and named in West Union. The area was renamed Groesbeck in 1857 when the post office was established; several other towns with the same name already existed in Ohio. The name Groesbeck comes from William Groesbeck, a former US House member from the area. The community was known for its commercial activity, specifically the establishment of two popular taverns and hotels at the intersection of Colerain and Galbraith Roads. The taverns went through several ownership and name changes through the years, eventually becoming Hotel Keller, and Frey's. These two establishments were helpful to the many farmers and ranchers who were driving their livestock down Colerain Pike to the slaughterhouses in Cincinnati.[28] They gave shelter to both the farmers and the livestock by providing barns as well. Many political gatherings and rallies were held at the establishments over the years. Groesbeck also hosted the area's first Improvement Association, which in turn formed the Groesbeck Fire Department as a separate entity in 1931.[29] Today Groesbeck is a bustling suburban community, hosting many businesses and homes.

Bevis

This community was named after one of the chief residents of the township and his family, Jesse Bevis. The village was established south of Georgetown/Dunlap

---

[27] Wells, 59
[28] Wells, 20
[29] Wells, 59

on Old Colerain Road in 1816. After making reportedly $400 from selling farm produce in New Orleans, Bevis established a village with a log, and later brick, hotel/tavern serving as the center of the community. He also built a gristmill and distillery on some of his property, which the Blue Rock Creek ran through. A new tavern was built when the Colerain Turnpike was constructed in the mid-1800's. The new tavern/hotel was built and dedicated in 1855. In 1920, the brick structure was torn down. This building stood roughly where I-275 crossed Colerain Ave.[30]

Pleasant Run

Pleasant run is located in the northern section of the township about a half-mile south of the border from Butler County. It takes its name from a small stream of the same name in the area.[31] Stories from the early history of the area include a Native American attack, where Native Americans ambushed Corporal Michael Hahn and two other soldiers while they were taking a cow out to Fort Dunlap. Another story relates the ambush of Colonel Robert Elliot, who was acting as a contractor for Wayne's Army, taking supplies to Fort Hamilton. Native Americans killed Elliot while he was leading a wagon team with supplies. When one of the Native Americans tried to scalp Elliot, they pulled his hair back only to discover he had a wig. The disgusted Native American attacker reportedly said it "was a big lie". The Colonel's servant escaped and was killed when he tried to retrieve the body of his master. An armed party later left Fort Washington in Cincinnati, and retrieved both bodies and brought them back to the fort. The Colonel's body was buried in the old Fourth Street Presbyterian burying grounds, was later moved to the

---

[30] Wells, 19
[31] Wells, 23

cemetery on Twelfth Street,(now Washington Park), and is now buried in Spring Grove Cemetery.[32]

One of the early families in the area was the Huston Family. Samuel Huston settled sometime after 1795 in the Pleasant Run area after acquiring several large tracts of land. The current Pleasant Run Elementary and Pleasant Run Middle schools are built on land that was once owned by the Huston Family. Samuel's son James Huston was a distiller in the area and owned around 1500 acres of land surrounding Hamilton Pike. He was also a significant shareholder in the turnpike. Several other pioneer families include the Stout, Pottenger, Sloniker, Hughes, Struble, Martin, and Liechauer families.[33] Pippin Road and Hamilton Ave. are still some of the main roads to cross the area, Pippin Road being petitioned for in 1822. Pleasant Run today is a lively suburban community, supporting many businesses and homes. One of the largest subdivisions in the area is Pleasant Run Farms. Even though it is not located in Colerain Township, the neighborhood has brought much development to the Colerain village of Pleasant Run. Originally set as the fifth site for the Homerama building show in 1965, this neighborhood is located in neighboring Springfield Township and has over 1,200 homes and over 3,600 residents, adding to the suburban feel of the formerly rural area of Pleasant Run.[34]

White Oak

White Oak is an active community located in Colerain Township, bordered by Monfort Heights in Green Township to the south. A portion of White Oak lies within the boundaries of Green Township as well. In

---

[32] Wells, 23
[33] Wells, 25
[34] "History." Pleasant Run Farms Civic Association. http://www.pleasantrunfarms.org/history.html.

pioneer times, it received its name from the abundance of white oak trees that prospered in the area. White oak lumber was valued for its "tight cooperage," or the fact it made great material for kegs and barrels, and its wood is described as being "naturally plugged" so the wood is nonporous. The original settlers in the area were predominately German immigrants, who helped play a valuable role in the 1800's beer boom in Cincinnati, when brewing was one of many vital industries in the German dominated city. The area was first names St. Jacobs after the St. James Catholic Church still located in the area. Jacob is the German word for James. In the later 1800's the area was called Creedville after a post office that was situated at Blue Rock and Banning roads in Colerain Township. Currently, the Coleraine Historical Society is renovating the building and it is on display at Heritage Park. By the 1920's, the area was now called White Oak, harkening back to the first settlers who preferred the trees in the area for their trades and consumption.

<u>The Civil War comes to Colerain Township</u>
John Hunt Morgan was a General for the Southern Confederate Army and famous as a successful raider using guerilla war tactics not taught at many of the military academies where Napoleonic War tactics made up much of the curriculum. When he and his band of raiders threatened Colerain Township and the communities, the area went into a panic.[35] His actions created one of the scariest moments for many of the residents of the township during the civil war. Cincinnati during the Civil War was relatively isolated during much of the duration of the war. The areas surrounding Cincinnati read brief accounts of the war in the various newspapers, and heard stories from returning veterans,

---

[35] Mowery, David L. *Morgans Great Raid: The Remarkable Expedition From Kentucky to Ohio*. Charleston, SC: The History Press, 2013. 85

but didn't hear much else. Until the dread-filled days and nights of July 13-14, 1863 came and went, when Colerain Township's communities had a brush with the war the inhabitants did not want to encounter again. General John Hunt Morgan was leading raids through Kentucky on July 2, 1863. He ravaged Indiana, then Ohio. It was in Ohio that he brushed the Colerain Township community of Bevis. Going up parts of Springdale Rd, Morgan's troops seemed to be taunting the Union soldiers stationed in Cincinnati, a prominent industrial center for the Union war effort. Fear gripped the township as a portion of his raiders rode through the area on July 13, spent part of the night in the area, and moved on the next day.[36] Morgan and his men eventually surrendered in West Point Ohio on July 26, 1863.[37] On his way through Colerain Township, many residents dreaded the war and its impact that the raiders could be bringing to the area. Many first families of the township have their stories of the raid, passed down from one generation to the next, adding to the legend of the two fateful days the Civil War brushed by Colerain Townships communities.

---

[36] "The Morgan Raid." *Cincinnati Commercial Tribune*, July 14, 1863.
[37] Mowery, 162

This sign along Springdale Road marks the route taken by Morgan's Raiders through Colerain Township. This sign was installed in 2013 during celebrations commemorating the 150th anniversary of the raid. (Photo courtesy Joe Flickinger)

This photo shows Colerain Ave. and Struble Rd in the late 1950's. This photo is looking north. The buildings on the right were a Mobil Service Station in what would be Bevis. Today this is the site of the Rumpke offices. (Photo courtesy Coleraine Historical Society)

This photo shows Colerain Ave at Galbraith Road in 1910. The Groesbeck Hotel is on the right, and the Hotel Keller is on the left. Colerain Ave is still a gravel road. (Photo courtesy Coleraine Historical Society)

This photo shows the Groesbeck Hotel and Grocery owned by J. Frey located on the northeast corner of Colerain Pike and Galbraith Road. (Photo courtesy Coleraine Historical Society)

This photo shows how the intersection of Colerain and Galbraith roads looked in 1906. Galbraith Road runs left to right. The Keller Hotel is on the left, and the Groesbeck Hotel is on the right. (Photo courtesy Coleraine Historical Society)

This photo shows the Hotel Keller in the early 1900s with a motorcycle club lined up in front of the building. (Photo courtesy Coleraine Historical Society)

This photo shows the Creedville Toll House and Post Office which used to stand at Banning and Blue Rock Roads. Heritage Park in Colerain Township is the permanent home of the structure. Built in 1829, the Coleraine Historical Society is refurbishing the structure. (Photo by Joe Flickinger)

Chapter Four:
The Twentieth Century Brings Change

The onset of the "War to end all Wars", the automobile, the streetcar, and the telephone began to shrink the world as people knew it in the early 1900's. Cincinnati was enduring as a major Midwestern city. Its recovery from the Civil War was minimal- without any major battles in the Greater Cincinnati area; Cincinnati remained intact as a major city. The problems it had in the 1900s were corruption and stagnation. George "Boss" Cox and his political machine were doing their best to maintain control of the city and its government. In the meantime, life in Colerain Township before WWI continued as it had as major events occurred in other parts of the nation and world. Several of the township villages and hamlets gained post offices, which gave an opportunity for several new shops and taverns to open. Jesse Bevis opened the first post office in his Bevis Tavern in 1835. Dunlap established its post office in 1837, with David Wallace as its first postmaster. Pleasant Run welcomed a post office in 1845, with James Huston as its first postmaster. This post office was discontinued in 1907. In 1857, Groesbeck opened its post office with Martin Luichinger as its first postmaster. Alois Jutzi became the postmaster of the Barnesburg post office in 1874 and continued until 1905. The Creedville post office was established in 1880 in a toll house at Blue Rock and Hanley roads with Fridolon Gutzwiller as its first postmaster. It lasted until 1905. Taylor Creek also had a post office established in 1857, lasting until 1905 with John Davis as its first postmaster.[38] These rural outposts allowed the people of the area to have a place to come together and share news, swap stories, and buy goods or arrange for services for their farms. Many were located in taverns or hotels that allowed the proprietor to bring in more business and to diversify the products they offered.

---

[38] Wells, 55

Transportation

Transportation throughot the area was rough, to say the least. While Cincinnati enjoyed some form of horse-drawn streetcar system since the mid-1800's, Colerain Township did not have the opportunities that other parts of the city had. The roads were the biggest obstacle to travel. The roads through the early 1900's were not the smooth, steady, black-topped roads we all know today. The roads of Colerain Township since its inception were dirt, gravel, or macadam roads. The dirt roads progressed to either macadam or paved roads. Macadam roads were a combination of crushed rock and gravel. Township residents were required to donate a certain amount of time to roadwork, or to hire it out to other workers. With the sale of many of the private turnpikes to Hamilton County in the late 1800's, asphault replaced gravel. The prominent road through the area was Colerain Turnpike, established as a private turnpike in the 1830's. Colerain Pike ran from Brighton Corner inside of the city, through Colerain Township, crossed the Great Miami River, went through Venice(today's Ross), through Oxford Ohio and ended in Brookville Indiana. For many years it was known as the Colerain, Oxford, and Brookville Turnpike. The chief surveyor and engineer of this turnpike was Alfred Gilbert, whose name is used for Gilbert Ave in Cincinnati.[39] Colerain Pike became a major travel route for farmers driving their livestock to the city stockyards. The most common forms of livestock to travel early Colerain Pike included cattle, hogs, and even flocks of turkeys.[40] Several hotels and taverns were established along Colerain Pike through its early years becoming major stopovers for farmers and ranchers driving their stock to the city. Groesbeck hosted two such establishments located right across from one another. Luichingers, and Weisenhans along Colerain and present day Galbraith Rd. Among other events held

---

[39] Wells, 56
[40] Wells, 14

at these establishments, political rallies took place at both locations.[41] The Bevis Tavern had its beginnings in 1816 when Jesse Bevis helped name the town named after him. His tavern became a landmark in the area. The Six Mile House was a stopover for farmers and was named because it was six miles from the start of the turnpike located in the Cincinnati area called Brighton. Not much was known about its early years of operation, other than "several owners ran their respective businesses out of it, including Thadeus Olmstead, John Hatt, and Edward Foster all owned or operated their businesses out of the structure at one time."[42] Many of these early turnpikes had toll gates from which the companies that funded the construction of the road could collect their fees. These consisted of a small building for the toll keeper's comfort. Usually, the men employed at these crossings ate and slept in these buildings. Toll Keepers lived a solitary life without any traffic passing by for several days. The gates consisted of a strong, wooden pole, long enough to cross the road. A large wooden hinge attached to the wood pole and had a box of large stones for weight. The other end was attached by a large rope to the keeper's dwelling, which made it impossible for the traveler to go any further without paying their toll. Rocks lifted the unfastened rope until there was enough clearance for the traveler to proceed. The price of the toll was based on the mileage and the number of horses used to haul the load on their vehicles.[43]

A Railroad?

Many longtime residents have heard rumors of a railroad planned to run through the township. The

---

[41] Wells, 14
[42] Wells, 14
[43] Hermann-Craig, Rosella. *Our Heritage- Colerain Township.* Cincinnati, Ohio: Colerain Township Bicentennial Committee, 1976.

Cincinnati Western Railroad was to have run into downtown Cincinnati through the western hills of Groesbeck, the Green Township community of Mt. Airy, over West Fork Creek, through a tunnel in Rolls Hill, and enter Cincinnati through the Millcreek Valley. On February 10, 1851, the charter for the railroad was registered; it was to construct a standard gauge railroad from Cincinnati to Chicago. Due to the engineering costs of traversing the hills and steep curvatures, the line was abandoned in the late 1850's, with only several miles of roadbed that was graded; some is still visible today.[44]

Even Better...an Airport???

Many longtime residents of Colerain Township also remember the small airport located in what is today the parking lot of Northgate Mall. Established in 1927 by several area businessmen, the airport took the name Mt Healthy Airport due to a regulation at the time stating airports must take the name of the closest municipal entity for easier identification. Since Mt Healthy was the closest incorporated city or village, it lent its name to the airport. The airport complex was leased from the Bosserman family, who lived in the white building across the street on Springdale Road, which was until recently home to Vilas Reality. Further development in the area forced the demolition of the house. Like many of the smaller local airports of the time, the Mt Healthy Airport was a hub of activity for small pilot training flights, as well as small airmail flights. The airport was served by a short runway, which was dirt and grass. It became difficult to take off when the ground was soft and muddy, as the wheels kicked up dirt and mud that stuck to the underside of the airplane and wings, adding weight to the

---

[44] Jakucyk, Jeffrey . "Cincinnati Western Railroad." Cincinnati Traction History. http://jjakucyk.com/transit/cw.html.

plane during takeoff. The complex had two hangarsand an attached office. There was no radio for direction, only a windsock located outside the hangar. There was no other safety equipment other than a fire extinguisher.[45] The airport operated until roughly 1955 when smaller local airports found it difficult to compete with the larger regional and later international, airports. The area today is a parking lot for Northgate Mall, bordered on the northern edge of the Colerain Veterans Memorial and the busy intersection of Colerain Ave. and Springdale Rd.

A second airport was located on Pippin Road close to Adams Road. This hosted a flying school. Constructed in 1946, Lakewood Airport operated until 1956. Returning GI's received flying lessons on the GI Bill. The major occurrence at this airport was in 1953 when three F-86 Saber fighter jets had to emergency land their crafts at this tiny airstrip on their flight from Illinois to Wright Patterson Air Force Base in Dayton Ohio. The jets were dangerously low on fuel, and the pilots landed at the closest airstrip possible. Wright-Patterson sent mechanics to the tiny airstrip to modify the jets and take off any extra weight such as ammunition, and strapped extra rockets to assist with takeoff. The jets carried enough fuel to make it to the Cincinnati Airport in Northern Kentucky to be refitted with fuel and ammunition to make it back to Dayton.[46]

A third smaller airport operated close to where Walmart, Clippard Park, and I-275 cut through the area. This little airstrip, mainly used by the Clippard family, saw little action other than small planes going in and out, except for a near fatal accident in 1956 when two

---

[45] Scholle, Frank. "Mt. Healthy Airport." Cincinnati Aviation Heritage Society & Museum.
http://www.cahslunken.org/pages/MtHealthyStory.htm.
[46] "Four Jets in Forced Landing." Cincinnati Enquirer, January 15, 1953, Cincinnati ed., sec. 1.

members of the Clippard family crash landed on the strip.[47]

Colerain Cemeteries

There are many smaller cemeteries that dot the landscape of Colerain Township. These little cemeteries are the final resting place of the early settlers of Colerain Township. Often these early cemeteries were religious cemeteries attached to churches. Colerain Township cares for many of the smaller historic cemeteries. The township has also placed wooden signs at most of these old burial grounds, identifying them for future generations.

Dunlap Station Cemetery

This cemetery is located on East Miami River Road close to the area where Fort Dunlap once stood. Heritage Park borders the cemetery, believed to be the oldest burial ground for settlers in the township. Burials began somewhere in 1791 or shortly after since proper records either were not kept or have been lost. The earliest date on headstones goes back to 1801. Several burials made in this cemetery are believed to be from the original attack on Ft. Dunlap, including Abner Hunt who was tortured and killed as a way to try to convince the settlers in the fort to surrender, but no known definitive records exist to prove it. The cemetery includes the graves of several other men who were killed by Native Americans in the 1790's and veterans from the Revolutionary War, War of 1812, Mexican War, and the Civil War buried here.[48]

Huston Cemetery

A deed was recorded in 1810 for the Presbyterian Church of Colerain Township. So many members of the

---

[47]Scholle, Francis H., and Don Linz. Images of America: Colerain Township. Charleston, SC: Arcadia Pub., 2010, 95
[48] Wells, 57,

Huston Family are buried here that the cemetery has taken the name "Huston Cemetery." For many years, a small church stood there called "the Peoples Church." This cemetery is located on Kemper Road just west of Pippin next to the water tower.[49]

Compton Cemetery

Another early cemetery located in the township is the Compton Cemetery, located on Compton Road near Pippin Road. This burial ground has a stone that dates back to 1807. After his death in 1821, the cemetery became the burial site for Jacob Compton, a Revolutionary War Veteran. It became the burial site for numerous other Compton family members as well as other well-known families from the township including Monfort, Stout, Struble, and Weston.[50]

St Bernards Catholic Cemetery

This cemetery serves the Roman Catholic parishioners of St. Bernards Church at the intersection of Harrison Ave. and Springdale Road in Taylor Creek. The cemetery was established in 1867 with the parish. It is the last resting place for well-known residents from the area including Monges and Allgeier.[51]

St James Catholic Cemetery

This cemetery straddles the Colerain-Green Township border in the area known as White Oak. The area was once known as St Jacobs then later Creedville, but took the name White Oak after the abundance of white oak trees in the area. This cemetery was established in 1844 with the church on land donated by the Oehler family. The parish was the "mother church" for many of the earlier Catholic churches in southern

---

[49] Wells, 57
[50] Wells, 57
[51] Wells, 58

Colerain and northern Green townships. The church still operates the cemetery today. It is comprised of over twenty acres.[52]

Bevis-Cedar Grove Cemetery
    This cemetery, located on today's busy Colerain Ave, was established in 1870. Members of its first board of trustees included George Gosling, David Bevis, and Isaac Erven. Adjacent to this cemetery is a small Methodist cemetery on a small plot of land donated by Jesse Bevis. The Methodist Church built here is now a former Masonic Hall. Many pioneer families from the 1800's are buried in this cemetery. Remains from the tiny Hardin Cemetery were moved here in 1937 from the Hardin Farm on Springdale Road. James Hardin was a Revolutionary War Veteran who also served an early treasurer of Colerain Township. An original receiving vault, built in 1875, is still located within its grounds. Bevis-Cedar Grove is still operating today.

Crown Hill Cemetery
    This is the newest cemetery in Colerain Township and is located on Pippin Road in Pleasant Run. It was established by John Sinclair in 1966. A private corporation owns and operates it today. The cemetery is known for a replica of the Liberty Bell on display for all visitors to see.[53]

    Many of the smaller cemeteries located in Colerain Township are cared for by township. For a more comprehensive list see Appendix 2.

---

[52] Remler, Mary H., ed. Hamilton County, Ohio, Burial Records, Volume 10: Green Township. Vol. 10. Westminster, Maryland: Heritage Books, 2012, 157
[53] Wells, 58

The headstone of War of 1812 veteran Joseph Cilley at Dunlap Cemetery and is located next to the current Colerain Heritage Park, and near the site of Fort Dunlap. (Photo courtesy Coleraine Historical Society)

MEMORIAL SERVICES

2:00 p.m.

SUNDAY, MAY 25, 1969

EAST MIAMI RIVER RD.   ONE MILE SOUTH OF COLERAIN

DUNLAP STATION CEMETERY

DIRECTED BY THE

COLERAINE HISTORICAL SOCIETY
Incorporated

The Coleraine Historical Society has been involved in ceremonies honoring veterans and early inhabitants of the township since the 1960's at Dunlap Station Cemetery. This program was from Memorial Day 1969. (Photo courtesy Coleraine Historical Society)

This photo captures the sight of a Memorial Day ceremony held at Dunlap Station Cemetery and hosted by the Coleraine Historical Society. (Photo courtesy Coleraine Historical Society)

This photo shows the receiving vault at Bevis-Cedar Grove Cemetery on Colerain Avenue. During harsh weather, bodies were held in the buildings until they could dig the graves. This building dates back to 1875. (Photo by Joe Flickinger)

This 1856 map of Colerain Township shows the Cincinnati Western Railroad line going through the township on its way to Butler County. Logistics and lack of money prevented the railroad from being built. (Photo courtesy Coleraine Historical Society)

This photo shows the Mt. Healthy Airport in 1947 located at the southwest corner of Springdale and Colerain Ave. The dirt runway is located in the upper left of the photo. The area of the runway is now parking and restaurants for Northgate Mall, and the hangars are now the Colerain Memorial Plaza. (Photo courtesy Coleraine Historical Society)

This photo shows the three F-86 Saber jets that were forced to land at small Lakewood Airport in 1953 due to low fuel. This airport was located off Pippin Rd close to Adams Rd. (Photo courtesy Coleraine Historical Society)

In 1917, a mass commemorating the 50th anniversary of the founding of the St. Bernard Church was held. The church and school were not big enough to hold the crowd. The original church, pictured above, was replaced in 1935. St Bernard celebrated its 150th anniversary in 2017. (Photo courtesy St. Bernard Church)

Chapter Five:
Post War Growth: Farms to Subdivisions

The major historical events of WWI and WWII brought about the sad sight of sons, brothers, husbands, and fathers going off to war. Colerain Township played its part by sending many of its sons to fight in a war halfway around the world. WWI gave way to the 1920s, and life stayed the same in Colerain Township save the occasional horseless carriage or two bounding down the gravel roads. The increasing affordability of automobiles made commuting to Cincinnati an easier task. During the 1930s, Colerain Township joined the rest of the country in making it through the Great Depression. Economic growth slowed tremendously, and leaving the township to find a job in the city became a very attractive opportunity for second jobs. As WWII began, residents learned how to grow victory gardens and ration goods while sending their sons and husbands to Union Terminal to depart on trains to fight the Germans and Japanese. There was one constant- the rural way of life. Colerain Township experienced growth, but only a few houses at a time. However, the entire character of the township was about to change. Shortly after the end of WWII, the returning GI's needed housing provided from loans through the GI Bill. Many GI's did not want the noisy, busy, and often crime-prone city neighborhoods to serve as the home for their new families. In the late 1940s, the birth of the Baby Boom generation began and as a result, the areas once known as farming communities became prime targets for developers to build huge subdivisions to house the growing population. Colerain Township's population swelled because of the subdivisions which permanently changed the face of the township forever. Huge farms became new neighborhoods with small, cookie-cutter Cape Cods with two and three bedrooms, a one car garage and a fenced in backyard. The area's farms disappeared slowly. A new baby boom meant more cars, more kids, and, as a result, better roads and better schools.

Schools

Colerain Township schools have their roots in the old log cabins and one room school houses that one imagines from stories about pioneer education. Today's educational trends of mega schools, that resemble malls or office buildings rather than the one or two room schools of yesterday would amaze our first settlers. Early pioneers, so far removed from the City of Cincinnati and its opportunities, could never have imagined the need or cost involved with running the major school district Colerain Township supports today. The pioneers would also be amazed by the vast number of residents choosing to send their children to the many private schools within the township. Today, public school students attend the schools in the Northwest Local School District, which has the second largest number of students in Hamilton County. There are also some private and parochial schools which call Colerain Township home or draw students from the township.

It was ordered in the Congress of 1785 that every divided section or township in the Northwest Territory should have a portion cordoned off for public education. It was reaffirmed in the Ordinance of 1787.[54] It was later ordered that a section 16 in every Township had to be set aside for public education. Later, the order was repealed. In 1821, the first law was passed that allowed the levying of taxes for the support of local schools. This law also helped to set up the township system of schools, splitting up the local townships into "districts", as well as an early school "committee", which could be taken as an early form of a locally elected school board, which is the common way the public's voices are heard in the schools today.[55] The very first grammar and high schools in Hamilton

---

[54] Lewis, Wm G.W. *A Biography of Samuel Lewis, First Superintendant of Common Schools for the State of Ohio*, Cincinnati, Ohio, Methodist Book Concern Publishers, R.P. Thomson Printers 1857. 98
[55] Wells, 34

County considered "common" or accepted all students from the public, were Woodward Grammar and High School situated just north of the old courthouse in Cincinnati. Even though citizens did not pay taxes for the school, the fees were paid by William Woodward, a wealthy Cincinnatian who was a big supporter of common education. This venture proved very successful and provided a preview of the successes to come in public common schooling.[56]

Meanwhile, in Colerain Township, educational life went by slowly. State mandates were slow to reach rural areas such as Colerain Township and as a result, public schools such as Woodward were non-existent. With the passage of the 1821 law, small one and two room schools were built in the aforementioned districts. Colerain Township established schools when there were enough students in a district to warrant hiring a teacher. An 1827 report from Stewart McGill, Clerk of Colerain Township, lists students of Colerain Township as being divided up into several districts; later they were expanded and split before consolidation in 1924. District #1 was located in the southeast corner of the township. This is now the Groesbeck area. The district extended east to west from Pippin to Cheviot roads and northwest to Compton Road. District #2 was the next district north, going north of the intersection of Springdale and Colerain Ave, and west from the township line to Brehm Road. At times District #2 brought in parts of Compton, Cheviot, and Springdale roads. District #3 covered the Pleasant Run area. Its northern boundary was the county line between Hamilton and Butler counties and extended from Hughes Road to Hamilton Pike. District #4 was located in the Barnesburg area of the township. Its territory went from Brehm Road to Daleview. District #5 was the Bevis School. The school was located on Colerain Pike just south of Day Road. Its territory included most of Hughes and Dry Ridge roads. District #6 was nicknamed

---

[56] Lewis, 107-108

the "Cliptown" school. This school was located further up Colerain Pike and its territory included the Dunlap area, down to the Great Miami River, also including at times, parts of Butler County. District #7 was the Peach Grove School, and included much of Taylors Creek, as well as parts of Springdale Road, as well as Althaus and Forfeit Run roads. District #8 was the Blue Rock District and included Blue Rock Road. District #9 included Dry Ridge, Day, Gosling, and Owl Creek Roads.[57] Throughout the years several other districts were set up to address the growing number of students, including District #10, which was named the Dunlap School and was located on Stone Mill Road. District #11 , also called Mt. Vernon School, or "Big Woods" School, was set up along Harrison Ave in Taylor Creek in 1836 and stretched to the Great Miami River north into Thompson Road. District #12 was carved out of District #9 and included most of Harrison Pike to the Great Miami River as well as East Miami River Road.[58]

In 1922, the members of many of the districts began preparations for a bond issue to consolidate several of the small schools into one large school for the township. The School housed grades 1-12. The only high school was the Colerain Roundtop High School, which housed grades 9-11. Students wishing to finish their diploma had to attend Mt Healthy High School. In 1924, 371 students and nine teachers began in the brand new centralized school. The first class of nine students graduated in May of 1925. The first building, which is still in use today, currently houses grades Kindergarten through 5th grade. In 1931, thanks to additional families moving into the township, the original Colerain High School on Poole Road opened next to the original centralized school building. It housed grades 7-12, and gave students increased opportunities for clubs and sports, especially after the athletic boosters built the

---

[57] Wells, 34-35
[58] Wells, 35

original football field for use for the 1953 season. In 1949, the Colerain School district absorbed the Pleasant Run School District into the Colerain Consolidated School District. The Pleasant Run district was a one-room school district that had resisted joining the rest of Colerain Township in their consolidated schools in the 1920s. After losing several teachers in one year, the Hamilton County Board of Education recommended they join Colerain. When they joined, the total enrollment jumped to around 880 students.[59] By the 1950s, it became apparent with the influx of new families buying and building homes during the baby boom after WWII, that the school district needed new facilites. With the passage of bond issues, new buildings and one additional smaller school system were absorbed into the district. In 1959, the second elementary school to open was Struble Elementary, named after longtime teacher, principal, and the first Colerain Superintendent Clarence Struble.

In 1960, after the State of Ohio encouraged the continued consolidation of smaller districts into bigger ones, Monfort Heights School District in northern Green Township joined Colerain Consolidated Schools. The resulting merger prompted a name change from Colerain Consolidated to the Northwest Local School District.[60] This name reflects the area's historical legacy as being part of the original Northwest Territory. In 1960, Taylor Elementary opened and was named after former Colerain teacher, principal, and the district's 2nd superintendent, Harry Taylor. Mr. Taylor died suddenly in December of 1948, and this building was named in his honor. In 1962, White Oak Jr. High School opened to handle the population boom from Monfort Heights and White Oak. That same year, Pleasant Run Elementary opened as well. In 1964, the current Colerain High School opened, and the old high school building became Colerain Junior High School; and in 1965, Weigel Elementary, named

---

[59] Craig –Hermann, 31
[60] Scully, 9

after district teacher Ann Weigel, who taught township students for 46 years, also opened. In 1966, Houston Elementary opened, named for Ophelia Houston, another longtime teacher in the district. This building now serves as the Pre-School Building for the district, as well as the location of a centralized enrollment center for the district. In 1969, the current Pleasant Run Junior High School was built to ease overcrowding in the two junior high schools. The school district served over 13,000 students at that time. In 1970, Bevis Elementary opened, named after the one room school in the area, as well as the Bevis family. The district closed Bevis in 2013 due to declining enrollment. Also in 1970, the district began offering vocational programs.[61]

In 2007, the district partnered and merged with Butler Technology and Career Development School District to provide for a broad range of career and technical education programs. Students in the Northwest District have the opportunity to attend one of Butler Techs stand-alone campuses for programs, or they can enroll in one of the several programs still housed in Northwest or Colerain High Schools.[62] In 1972, with a district population nearing 15,000 pupils, Northwest Senior High School opened. This second high school relieved overcrowding issues at Colerain High School. In 1977, the district built Welch Elementary in the Pleasant Run Farms area to handle the influx of students from the Pleasant Run Farms subdivision. Welch was named after Everett J. Welch, the Assistant Superintendent who worked tirelessly for the passage of the bond issues in the 1970's providing funding for the construction of Bevis, Welch, and Northwest High School.

In 1999, a new bond issue passed, which allowed for the demolition and rebuilding of Monfort Heights

---

[61] Wells, 37
[62] "About the Northwest Local School District." Northwest Local School District. http://www.nwlsd.org/about/our-history--5/.

Elementary, originally built in 1930. This bond issue and levy included additions to both high schools, permitting additional academic classes and staff to be added. In 2010, the school district opened Northwest Passage across from the Transportation Office on Springdale Road. This program is an alternative educational environment for selected students from throughout the district.[63] In 2016, the Northwest District has seven elementary schools, three middle schools, and two high schools. Also, a pre-school building and an alternative school round out the major hubs of educational activities in Colerain Township. The Northwest District in 2016 had 707 certified/licensed staff, including both teachers and administrators, who serve a little over 9,300 students in grades pre-K to 12. This is in stark contrast to the 1924 opening of the consolidated school, where nine teachers in grades 1-12 taught 371 students![64]

Fire Protection

Colerain Township has a proud and long tradition of professional fire services provided to the residents of the area. However, before the 1930s, fire protection was sparse, to say the least. Some neighboring communities assisted in extinguishing fires, but response times and service was spotty. North College Hill, Fairfield, Ross, and New Baltimore were but a few departments who assisted if they could.[65] Bucket brigades handled small fires; however, as the population began to increase, albeit slowly, modern and reliable fire services became a necessity. In 1931, a large group of citizens from the Groesbeck area of the township met at Honnerts Garage

---

[63] Ibid
[64] Ibid
[65] Wells, 59, 62

on Colerain Avenue. They called their group the Groesbeck Improvement Association. It was at this meeting they decided to improve the safety of the area through fire protection. As a way to fundraise for this goal, they held a carnival in 1933 coinciding with the opening of a new road. They raised enough money to purchase a used Model A Ford Pumper. Throughout the years, many dances and other fundraising events were held to raise funds for the fire department, helping to protect the rapidly growing southern end of Colerain Township.[66]

   In 1954, the Colerain trustees began planning for a volunteer fire department to serve the northern end of the township, based in Dunlap. The first meetings consisted of planning for many raffles and other fundraising events, and necessary to establish and maintain a volunteer fire department at that time. Throughout the years, the Dunlap and Groesbeck volunteer fire departments grew in size and scope along with the township, each adding more services such as life squad services, increasingly more state of the art pumpers and fire engines, and continuing education for the firefighters. In 1975, the Groesbeck and Dunlap departments merged, forming the Colerain Township Fire Department.[67] In 1984, the volunteer system was abandoned, and paid employees were hired.[68] Today's fire department is an all-professional unit, with both full and part-time firefighters, EMT's, and paramedics. It maintains five stations, five first out engines, one spare engine, one 110' ladder, two water tankers, one heavy rescue, two rescue boats, four front line squads, three backup squads, two paramedic units and the Hamilton County Hazardous Materials response truck. The

---

[66] Wells, 59-60
[67] Wells, 62-63
[68] Colerain Fire Department website, http://www.colerain.org/department/fire/about-colerain-fire-dept/

department also has 53 career firefighter/paramedics (this includes all officers), one career mechanic, one career administrative assistant, and 110 part-time firefighters/EMT/paramedics. Colerain Township Fire Department has an extensive training division, public safety division (which includes fire inspections and public education), fire investigation unit, vehicle repair and maintenance garage, and citizen's fire academy.[69] Today's modern department is significantly different from the volunteer departments who served a much smaller, more rural population at its beginnings. The township's residents are lucky to have such a full fire/rescue division available at a moment's notice in case of an emergency.

Police Protection

      Police protection in Colerain Township from its founding until the mid-1800s remained sporadic at best. Hamilton County Sherriff deputies rarely patrolled rural areas such as Colerain Township, venturing into the hard to reach areas of Colerain only to serve warrants or to investigate crimes at the request of individual municipalities. Many townships such as Colerain simply did not have the money or the workforce to incorporate their police forces. Colerain Township from time to time employed part-time constables. One such instance was the use of constables to assist in transporting prisoners from one town or jurisdiction to the next. This could prove to be dangerous work, as was the case for one of Colerain's part-time constables in 1918. John Willsey was working part-time for the township escorting prisoners through the area. On August 15, 1918, Orville Ogg ambushed the constable in his home and shot him over money the constable had stored there. Willsey's name was later added to the National Law Enforcement

---

[69] Ibid

Memorial in Washington D.C. in 2008.[70] This rare yet horrendous act for the area at that time shows that no matter the place or period, law enforcement is a dangerous profession.

Unfortunately, due to the lack of funding and manpower, local citizens left smaller crimes for a constable to handle, or a justice of the peace was able to help. Many rural townships in Ohio utilized volunteer groups called "Anti-Thieving Associations" and "protective associations" to help in the fight against livestock or other minor thefts and felonies. Colerain Township had their own, which merged with the Springfield Township version, called the "Colerain-Springfield Protective Association." This group was instrumental in bridging the gap in law enforcement in rural areas such as Colerain Township. Members spread throughout the area whenever offenses were reported, sometimes setting up roadblocks to help catch a perpetrator or suspect. As the countryside welcomed more residents, these groups were deputized Special Deputies by the Hamilton County Sherrif's office throughout the 1940s and 1950s. As the groups were deputized, their organizations disappeared as was the case with Colerain. In the late 1940s, the township once again began to employ on a regular basis two part-time constables to handle traffic issues, minor criminal complaints, and help to serve warrants.[71]

In 1966, the township promoted William Terrell to be the first Chief Constable. He worked "part-time", usually in the evenings, at 50-60 hours a week.[72] It was under Terrell's leadership that Colerain Trustees formed a police district and a full-time police department in

---

[70] Weathers, William A. "Constable Honored- 89 Years late." Cincinnati Enquirer, May 8, 2008, NW ed., Your Hometown sec.
[71] Olvey, Patrick. History of the Colerain-Springfield Protective Association. Report. Cincinnati, Ohio, 2011.
[72] "Former Township Police Chief dies following Heart Attack." Cincinnati Enquirer, October 21, 1980, Suburbia in Brief sec.

1976.[73] Throughout the 1980s and 1990s, the township slowly built its police department to try to meet the policing needs of a booming suburban population. After a joint service agreement that provided the township with several patrol deputies and access to some of the auxiliary services ended with the Hamilton County Sheriff's office in 2014, the township police department further expanded their services to the public to include investigations and an impound lot. The police department today includes 54 full-time officers, five Sergeants, two Lieutenants, and one Chief. Also, six civilian staff members handle clerical and other administrative work. The department's other services include three school resource officers, one school investigator, two D.A.R.E. officers, six full-time Detectives, three Undercover officers, and one canine officer. The township also maintains a bike patrol, impound lot, complete traffic safety unit, CARE program for special needs citizens, block watches, a quick response team with the fire department, and a family justice center.[74] The services provided to the citizens of today's Colerain Township are a far cry to the days of part-time constables, whose main concern was traffic tickets and investigating small complaints of rural residents of the area. The citizens of Colerain Township are very lucky to have a comprehensive police department that can respond at a moment's notice to the needs of its diverse citizens.

    Colerain Township's police, firefighters, and educators serve the population with pride and excellence. They have a long history and take great strides to excel in their service to the population. All three organizations continue to grow and adapt to the needs of the community.

---

[73] "2 Tax levies seen losing." Cincinnati Enquirer, November 3, 1976, Suburban News sec.
[74] "Police." Colerain Township. http://www.colerain.org/department/police/.

This undated photo shows Colerain Constable John Willsey. Willsey was shot and killed in 1918 over money he had at his house. His name has been added to the National Law Enforcement Memorial in Washington D.C. (Photo courtesy Colerain Police Department)

This badge represents one of many protective groups whose mission was to help ensure that thefts and other small crimes were kept at a minimum in rural places like Colerain Township. (Photo courtesy Coleraine Historical Society)

This photo shows the badges after the merger of the Colerain and Springfield township protective associations. (Photo courtesy personal collection of Patrick Olvey)

Members of the Groesbeck Fire Department wore this badge. The Groesbeck and Dunlap departments later merged into the Colerain Fire Department. (Photo Courtesy Coleraine Historical Society)

This early photo shows members of the Groesbeck Fire Department in front of their station on Colerain Ave. (Photo courtesy Coleraine Historical Society)

George Matt owned the Dunlap Garage, located at Colerain and W. Kemper Rd. Later, this became the headquarters for the Dunlap Fire Department. (Photo courtesy Coleraine Historical Society)

This shows the program for the cornerstone laying of the new consolidated school taking place in September 1923. The building in the program above is still in use today as Colerain Elementary. (Courtesy Coleraine Historical Society)

This photo shows the students and staff of the newly opened Colerain Consolidated School in 1925. (Photo courtesy Coleraine Historical Society)

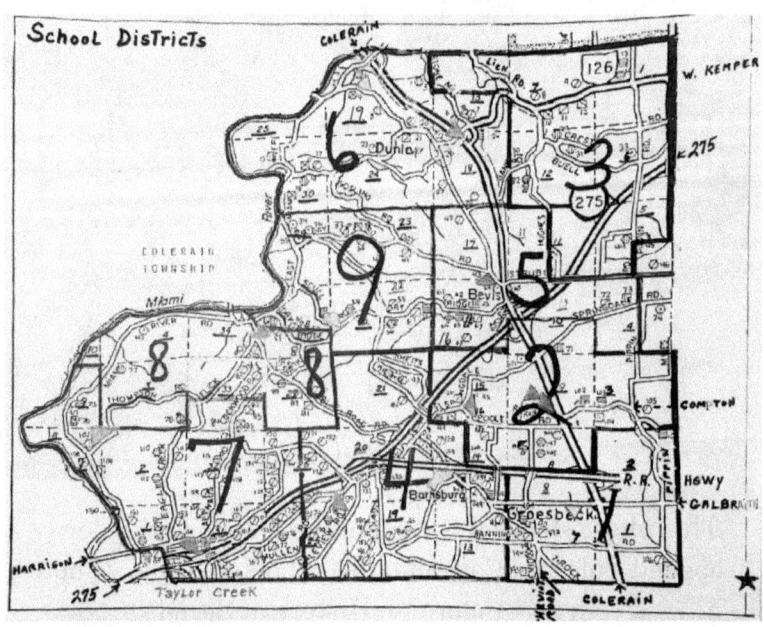

This map shows the general outline of the "old" township school districts where Colerain school children attended one or two room schools before their merger into the Colerain Consolidated Schools in 1923. (Map courtesy Coleraine Historical Society)

This photo shows the old Pleasant Run School located at Pippin and Crest roads. The small Pleasant Run district merged into the Colerain Consolidated School District in 1940. (Photo courtesy Coleraine Historical Society)

This photo shows the old Blue Rock School located on Blue Rock Rd near the intersection with East Miami River Road. In the early 1900s, the school would later accommodate students from the Barnesburg School. (Photo courtesy Coleraine Historical Society)

This photo shows an old Colerain Consolidated Schools school bus. These early buses often were converted farm trucks. (Photo courtesy Coleraine Historical Society)

First Annual Commencement

of the

Colerain Township High School

to be held in

The School Auditorium

on

Friday evening, June 5, 1925
at eight o'clock

PROGRAM

Music .... Colerain Orchestra
Invocation .... Rev. Stoehling
Vocal Solo .... Mr. Fred Schoffler
Class Address .... Mr. Meyers Y. Cooper
Vocal Solo .... Mr. Fred Schoffler
Presentation of Diplomas.. Ass't. Supt. W. F. Sizelove
Music .... Colerain Orchestra
Duet .... Miss Messinger and Mr. Schoffler
Benediction .... Rev. Van Saun

CLASS ROLL

Helen E. Craig	Alfred G. Huttles
Helen L. Hoock	George R. Ruoff
Mildred O. Shaw	Howard E. Hoock
Lourine M. Kraus	Robert E. Foster
Richard E. Joyce	

Class Colors: BLUE AND GOLD.
Class Flower: AMERICAN BEAUTY.
Class Motto: "TINT YOUR OWN SKY"

O. H. Bennett .... County Superintendent
W. F. Sizelove .... Assistant County Superintendent
C. A. Struble .... Principal
Harry E. Taylor   Dorothy M. Kress

BOARD OF EDUCATION

Christ Ruehl, President	George Schreimer
Geo. K. Foster, Clerk	Jacob Rutz
Elmer Weil	Christ Siebert

Hilltop Publishing Co.   M. Mt. Healthy, Ohio

This photo shows the program for the first graduation commencement of the Colerain Consolidated Schools in 1925. (Photo courtesy Coleraine Historical Society)

This photo shows Colerain High School in 2017. Built in 1964, this is the second building to use the name Colerain High School. In 1970 a vocational building was built, as well as in 1999 an addition to the main building was constructed. (Photo courtesy Joe Flickinger)

This picture shows Northwest High School under construction. This building was the second high school built in the booming Northwest Local School District. It was built in the early 1970s to relieve overcrowding conditions at Colerain High School. (Photo courtesy Northwest High School Library)

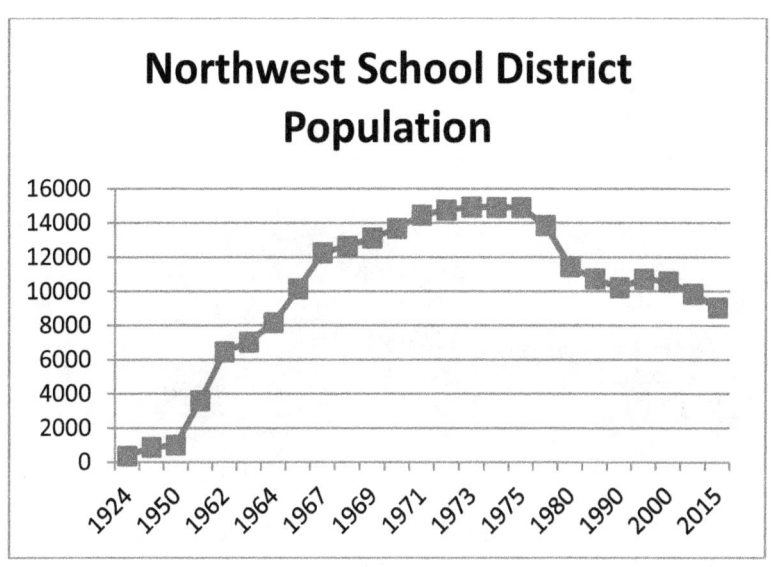

This chart shows the population growth of the Northwest Local School District since its establishment in 1924. In 1924 the student population was 371, peaking in 1973 at 14, 914, and currently at around 9,300 in 2016. The drop in students in the 1980's reflects increasing educational options for students in the Cincinnati area, including private, religious, and charter schools. (Data courtesy Coleraine Historical Society and Ohio Department of Education)

This photo shows the new Pleasant Run building site in August 2017. This building is part of an effort in the district to replace aging and outdated facilities. If construction continues as planned, the school should open in August 2018. (Photo courtesy Joe Flickinger)

**Chapter Six:
Looking Ahead to the Future**

As Colerain Township residents look back over 222 years of growth, modernization, and change, the township is poised to continue through the 21st century to reach 300 years of existence with much hope, promise, and potential, as well as fortitude to face the challenges change brings. The next 78 years should be very exciting.

The year 2017 marked continuous growth for the township. The many changes made to Colerain Ave. have begun to take shape. Changes to the Colerain-Springdale intersection has improved traffic flow, transforming the area into a gathering place, anchored by the Colerain Township Memorial Plaza located at the edge of Northgate Mall. The Coleraine Historical Society has many unique events planned, including the refurbishing of an old toll booth, the marking of the site of Fort Dunlap in the Colerain Heritage Park, as well as the marking of the highest flood level along the Great Miami River. The continued growth and popularity of German cultural groups headquartered in the township have brought a smile to the faces of many township residents as they hold their annual festivals and craft shows. Oktoberfest, Kristkindle Market, and sausage making are but a few of the wonderful community events that make up this vast contingent of the greater Cincinnati area that has claimed Colerain Township as their "home."

The revamping and addition of shopping and dining options to the area create new and exciting options that bring visitors and revenue to the area. Northgate Mall has been remodeled and expanded, with the addition of new stores and a movie theater providing shopping and entertainment opportunities not seen in quite a while. The Northgate Mall, which opened in the early 1970's on the site of the former Mt. Healthy Airport, experienced a major renovation in the early 2000s in response to changes in the retail industry. A new owner oversaw investment into more entertainment options such as the Xscape Theatre, adding stores such as Ulta, Burlington

Coat Factory, DSW Shoes, Marshalls, and Michaels, as well as numerous improved dining options including First Watch, Pot Belly, Cheddars, Longhorn Steakhouse as well as an updated McDonalds restaurant. A new outdoor shopping and dining development opened alongside the exit/entrance ramp to I-275 named Stonecreek Towne Center in 2007.[75] This new shopping and dining attraction includes a Best Buy, Meijer, Old Navy, and J.C. Penny's. It also features dining experiences like Olive Garden, Quaker Steak and Lube, Five Guys, and local favorite Larosa's Pizza. Colerain Ave. has seen the growth of newer businesses along the busy business corridor, as well as already established businesses, such as Dicks Sporting Goods, building bigger, more modern stores.[76] New housing and street rehabilitations occur every year, as well as the addition of Heritage Park, a new park located on the site of Fort Dunlap on East Miami River Rd further improving the already livable conditions in Colerain Township.

In 2015, the Northwest Local School District passed an operating/bond issue to consolidate and build three new elementary buildings, as well as renovate the middle and high schools. This action, along with the continued improvement in the classroom instruction is expected to help sustain the growth and positive feelings in Colerain Township for several years, as well as attract newer families to the area. After demolition of the old school buildings, the sites will be marketed to developers with an eye on building new single-family homes.

One looming issue the township needs to tackle is the aging housing stock in the older subdivisions. The older housing requires money to keep the structures up to

---

[75] Beyer, Mike. "JC Penny to Open Stonecreek Saturday." Cincinnati Enquirer, July 25, 2007, Business sec.
[76] Key, Jennie. "Dicks Sporting Goods Grand Reopening July 9th." Northwest Press(Cincinnati), July 6, 2016.

standards enjoyed by newer housing. Making sure the residents can keep their housing in excellent condition has been the goal of some new ideas such as a maintenance code which was enacted in 2007. These new codes help to identify and contribute to maintaining what would have become nuisance properties.

Keeping the township a "livable" suburb of Cincinnati must be addressed in order to continue to attract young families to the area. In the early 2000's exurbs such as Mason, West Chester, and Little Miami grew from a farming community to a major exurban part of the Greater Cincinnati area. An exurb is a suburban area established outside of the "beltway" interstates surrounding larger midwestern cities. These areas created a significant population drain on Hamilton County and many individuals left the county to pursue the wide open spaces with their newer homes and low taxed municipalities which are still run as if they were farming communities. Colerain Township needs to keep improving its roads to alleviate congestion, sewers to keep up with demand, and parks and recreation to help keep Colerain Township residents secure in the knowledge that their needs are being met.

In the meantime, businesses seem to be growing and thriving in the township. Besides the malls, and new chain stores moving in to establish their businesses, many old businesses are flourishing. Businesses such as Stehlins Meats, which harkens back to a time when meat markets and butchers were more common, continues to grow and produce high-quality products. Hams, sausages, ground beef, and local Cincinnati delicacies such as goetta round out the many food options available to Colerain residents at Stehlins, dating back to 1913 when business founder John Stehlin began slaughtering animals for the people who lived in the Bevis community.[77] Stehlins today is still a step back in time, when employees knew you and what your family bought. Customer service is still the most important part of the business besides good quality food. Farbach-Werner Nature Preserve is a part of the Hamilton County Park System. Nestled along the busy Colerain Ave. corridor in Groesbeck, the 23 acre property includes walking trails, and a house and barn that date back to the 1830's. The park is a quiet respite from the hustle of the 21st century.[78]

     Rumpke Waste & Recycling has kept and grown its headquarters in Colerain Township and increased its holdings to include recycling to complement its waste hauling business. Established in the 1930's, the waste hauling business began when the Rumpke family collected food scraps from area residents to feed the pigs on the family farm. In 1945 the family moved their farm to 80 acres in rural Colerain Township. In 1955, the family left the pig business and concentrated on waste disposal. Rumpke has introduced recycling, hydraulics, and portable restrooms to their business over the last 40 years. Today, Rumpke continues to expand into other areas of the country, owning and operating several landfills in other parts of the region.[79]

     Still, other businesses are proving their business practices will stand the test of time. Neidhard-Minges Funeral Home is one of those businesses. The funeral home began in 1860 in the home of Andrew Neidhard on Harrison Ave along Taylor Creek, straddling the border of northern Green Township and Southern Colerain Township. The funeral home celebrated its 150th

---

[77] Key, Jennie . "Family business has long history." Cincinnati Enquirer, May 23, 2013, Hometown sec.
[78] Wells, 67
[79] "Rumpke - Our Story." Rumpke - Our Story http://www.rumpke.com/about-us/our-story.

anniversary serving the people of southern Colerain Township in 2010, with six generations of the family having worked at the business, while maintaining other locations such as their headquarters in Westwood as well as a location in Harrison Ohio.

The next 78 years will bring much change. What will the men and women of the area say about Colerain Township at the 300th anniversary of its founding?

This undated photo shows workers on an old Rumpke Collection truck relaxing after a hard day of waste collection. Today, Rumpke is a major employer in Colerain Township. (Photo courtesy Rumpke Waste and Recycling)

The original Neidhard-Minges Funeral home as it appears today on Harrison Ave. at Taylor Creek in extreme southern Colerain Township. The building dates to the mid-1800s, becoming a funeral home since 1910. (Photo courtesy Neidhard-Minges Funeral home)

In 1978, the dedication of the Cincinnati Donauschwaben Hall and Clubhouse on Dry Ridge Road took place. This is one of several German Heritage groups calling Colerain Township home. (Photo courtesy Cincinnati Donauschwaben Society)

This photo shows the Natures Niche Gift Center in Farbach-Werner Park on Colerain Ave. This building was originally the home of David Williamson. The 23 acre property was donated by the Farbach-Werner family to Hamilton County Parks in 1972. (Photo courtesy Joe Flickinger)

This photo shows John "Butch" Stehlin posing in front of one of the trucks used for the family business in 1924. Stehlins Meats still provides quality product with personal service in 2017. (Photo courtesy Stehlins Meats)

This marker is currently the only remembrance of the fort and battle that took place at Fort Dunlap. The Coleraine Historical Society plans to raise funds to outline the "footprint" of the old fort recreated from old sketches and maps. This plaque stands near where the fort stood in what is now Heritage Park in Colerain Township.
(Photo by Joe Flickinger)

Appendix 1

Women who served Colerain Township in Elected Positions:

Anna Rinckel-Township Clerk, 1937
Henrietta Herrmann-Township Clerk, 1939
Helen Abercrombie-Township Trustee, 1976-77
Garnet Bernhardt-Township Trustee, 1982-85
Kathy Mohr-Township Fiscal Officer, 1988-2003
Patricia Clancy-Township Trustee, 1988-1997
Diana Rielage-Township Trustee, 1998-2005
Heather Harlow-Township Fiscal Officer, 2004-2017
Melinda Rinehardt-Township Trustee, 2012-2015

Appendix 2

List of Colerain Township Cemeteries

Barnes Family
Bethel
Bevis-Cedar Grove
Cloud
Colerain Township
Compton
Crawford
Crown Hill
Dean
Dunlap Station
Foster
Franklin Methodist
German United Brethren Church(Old)
Hammitt
Hardin
Huston
Ogg
Olive Branch Methodist
Richards-Gilbert

St. Bernard Catholic Church
St. James White Oak Catholic Church
St. John the Baptist Catholic Church
St. Paul Evangelical Lutheran Church
Schluniger
Smith
Trinity Lutheran Church
United Brethren Methodist(Old)
Van Sickle
West Branch of the Mill Creek Valley Baptist Church
White Oak Christian Church
White Oak Township
Willsey

Coleraine Historical Society has a list of all known names buried in many of these cemeteries

Appendix 3

Some township jobs have come and gone. Many positions were eliminated or combined into other jobs. Listed below are several jobs and the people who filled them in the early decades of Colerain Township.

Overseer of the Roads:
George Struble
HH Hughes
William Williamson

Constable
Joseph Struble
Joseph Day
Asher Williamson
Samuel Campbell

Petit Juror
Jonathon Cilley

Justice of the Peace
Isacc Sparks
Thomas Taylor

Jurors
Jonathan Cilley
James Struble

Clerk
John Dunlap

Overseer of the Poor
John Shaw

Viewers of Enclosures and Appraisers of Damages
Isacc Gibson
Samuel Cresswell
John Davis

Appendix 4

Roads named for early township officials.

Wiley(Willey)

Stout

Bevis

Huston

McGill

Adams

Struble

Compton

Hughes

Pottenger

Lockwood Hill

Bibliography

"2 Tax levies seen losing." Cincinnati Enquirer, November 3, 1976, Suburban News sec.

"A $5000 Blaze." *The Venice Graphic* (Venice Ohio), September 16, 1887.

"About the Northwest Local School District." Northwest Local School District. http://www.nwlsd.org/about/our-history--5/

Beyer, Mike. "JC Penny to Open Stonecreek Saturday." Cincinnati Enquirer, July 25, 2007, Business sec.

Cincinnati: An Urban Sourcebook Volume 2. Cincinnati Ohio, Cincinnati Historical Society, 1988

Colerain Fire Department website, http://www.colerain.org/department/fire/about-colerain-fire-dept/

Colerain Township Webpage, (accessed 3/26/2014) http://www.colerain.org

Cone, Stephen Decater, "Indian Attack on Fort Dunlap." *Ohio History*. Ohio Historical Society. 1887

Flanaghan, Deirdre & Laurence; *Irish Place Names*. Gill & Macmillan, 2002

Ford, Henry and Kate, *History of Hamilton County Ohio with Illustrations and Biographical Sketches*, Cleveland Ohio, L.A. Williams Publishers, 1881

"Former Township Police Chief dies following Heart Attack." Cincinnati Enquirer, October 21, 1980, Suburbia in Brief sec.

"Four Jets in Forced Landing." Cincinnati Enquirer, January 15, 1953, Cincinnati ed., sec. 1.

Hermann-Craig, Rosella. *Our Heritage- Colerain Township*. Cincinnati, Ohio: Colerain Township Bicentennial Committee, 1976

"History." Pleasant Run Farms Civic Association. http://www.pleasantrunfarms.org/history.html

Jakucyk, Jeffrey. "Cincinnati Western Railroad." Cincinnati Traction History. http://jjakucyk.com/transit/cw.html

Key, Jennie. "Dicks Sporting Goods Grand Reopening July 9th." Northwest Press(Cincinnati), July 6, 2016

Key, Jennie . "Family business has long history." Cincinnati Enquirer, May 23, 2013, Hometown sec.

Knepper, Dr. George, *The Official Ohio Lands Book* , Columbus Ohio, Auditor of the State of Ohio Publication, 2002

Kramb, Edwin A. *Buckeye Battlefields*. Springboro, OH: Valhalla Press, 2006

Lewis, Wm G.W. *A Biography of Samuel Lewis, First Superintendent of Common Schools for the State of Ohio*, Cincinnati, Ohio, Methodist Book Concern Publishers, R.P. Thomson Printers 1857

Mowery, David L. *Morgans Great Raid: The Remarkable Expedition from Kentucky to Ohio*. Charleston, SC: The History Press, 2013.

Olvey, Patrick. History of the Colerain-Springfield Protective Association. Report. Cincinnati, Ohio, 2011.

"Police." Colerain Township. http://www.colerain.org/department/police/

Remler, Mary H., ed. Hamilton County, Ohio, Burial Records, Volume 10: Green Township. Vol. 10. Westminster, Maryland: Heritage Books, 2012

"Rumpke - Our Story." Rumpke - Our Story http://www.rumpke.com/about-us/our-story.

Scamyhorn, Richard, and John Steinle. Stockades in the Wilderness: the Frontier Defenses & Settlements of Southwestern Ohio, 1788-1795. Dayton, Ohio: Landfall Press, 1986.

Scholle, Frank. "Mt. Healthy Airport." Cincinnati Aviation Heritage Society & Museum, http://www.cahslunken.org/pages/MtHealthyStory.htm

Scholle, Francis H., and Don Linz. Images of America: Colerain Township. Charleston, SC: Arcadia Pub., 2010

Scully, Henry, ed, *Remember When...Monfort Heights*, Cincinnati Ohio, Monfort Heights Civic Association, 1977

Silberstein, Iola, *Cincinnati, Then and Now*, Cincinnati, League of Women Voters, 1982

Steinman III, Phillip, *Beechwood Flats*, New York NY, Vantage Press, 1960

"The Morgan Raid." *Cincinnati Commercial Tribune*, July 14, 1863.

Tolzmann, Don Heinrich, *German Heritage Guide to the Greater Cincinnati Area,* Milford Ohio, Little Miami Publishing, 2003

Weathers, William A. "Constable Honored- 89 Years late." Cincinnati Enquirer, May 8, 2008, NW ed., Your Hometown sec.

Wells, Ruth, *Colerain Township Revisited, 1794-1994.* Cincinnati Ohio, Coleraine Historical Society, 1994

Index

Index

Abercrombie, Helen...107
Bernhardt, Garnet...107
Bevis, David...55
Bevis, Jesse...34,48,50,55
Campbell, Samuel...109
Cilley, Jonathan...109
Cilley, Joseph...57
Clancy, Patricia...107
Compton, Jacob...54
Cox, George...48
Creswell, Samuel...109
Davis, John...109
Day, Joseph...109
Denman, Mathias...4
Dunlap, John...5,8,12,33,109
Elliot, Colonel Robert...35
Erven, Isaac...55
Foster, Edward...50
Frey, J...42
Gibson, Isaac...109
Gilbert, Alfred...49
Girty, Simon...5
Gosling, George...55
Groesbeck, William...34
Gutzwiller, Fridolin...48
Hahn, Corporal Michael...35
Hamilton, Alexander...10
Hardin, Samuel...16
Harlow, Heather...107
Harrison, William Henry...32

Hatt, John...50
Herrmann, Henrietta...107
Houston, Ophelia...71
Hughes, H.H...109
Hunt, Abner...6,7,53
Huston, James...36
Huston, Samuel...36
Jutzi, Alois...48
Kingsbury, Lieutenant Jacob...5,6,7
Luichinger, Martin...48
Maner, William...28
Matt, George...83
McGill, Stewart...68
Mohr, Kathy...107
Morgan, General John Hunt...37,38
Muehlenhard, Robert...13
Ogg, Orville...74
Olmstead, Thadeus...50
Patterson, Robert...4
Richardson, Giles...26
Rielage, Diana...107
Rinckel, Anna...107
Rinehardt, Melinda...107
St. Claire, Arthur...10
Shaw, John...109
Sinclair, John...55
Stehlin, John...98
Steinman III, Phillip...21
Stites, Benjamin...4,9
Struble, Clarence...70
Struble, George...33
Struble, James...109
Struble, Joseph...109

Symmes, John
Cleves...4,5,8,9,10
Symmes, Timothy...10
Taylor, Harry...70
Terrell, William...75
Truman, Captain
Alexander...7
Wallace, David...48
Wallace, John...7
Washington, George...4
Weigel, Ann...71

Welch, Everett...71
West, Charles...34
West, Rebecca...17
Whittier, John
Greenleaf...26
Williamson, Asher...109
Williamson,
William...109
Willsey, John...74,78
Wiseman, William...7

About the Author

Joe Flickinger is a lifelong resident of the Cincinnati area. Joe holds a BA in History and an M.Ed in Educational Administration from Xavier University, and has partially completed an MA in Public History from Southern New Hampshire University. Joe has worked as a history teacher in Cincinnati for over 16 years. He serves as Vice-President of the Green Township Historical Association, and is a member of the Coleraine Historical Society. Joe maintains professional memberships in the American Historical Association, National Council of History Education, Organization of American Historians, National Council on Public History, and the American Association for State and Local History. He is married to his wonderful wife Kathleen, and has three beautiful children.

www.ingramcontent.com/pod-product-compliance
Lightning Source LLC
Chambersburg PA
CBHW070456090426
42735CB00012B/2578